Fashion Template Sketchbooks

© Fashion Template Sketchbooks
Cover illustration and fashion poses by Basak Tinli. Please do not copy and/or reproduce the artwork in any form. No part of this book may be reproduced, distributed, or transmitted by any means without the permission of the publisher. All rights reserved.

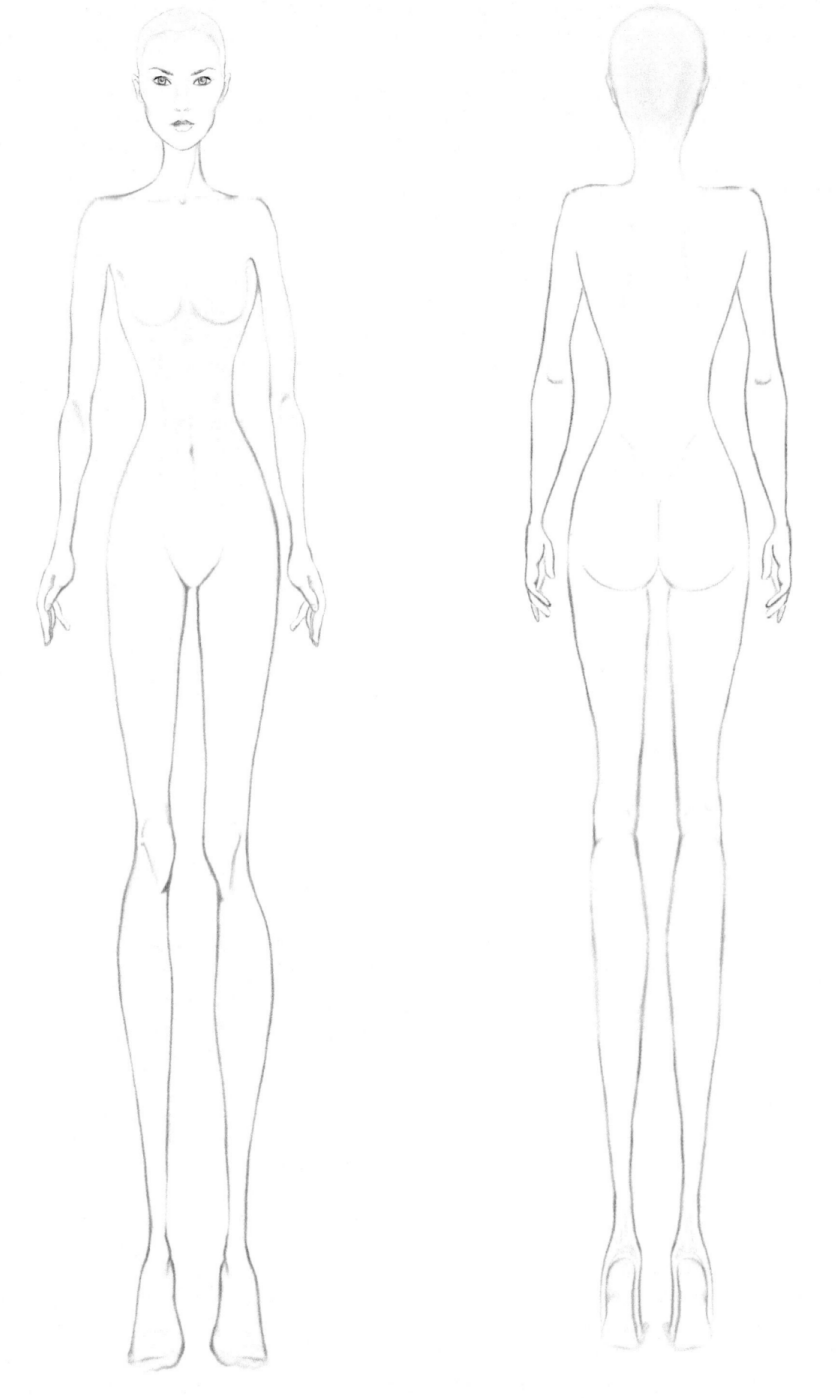

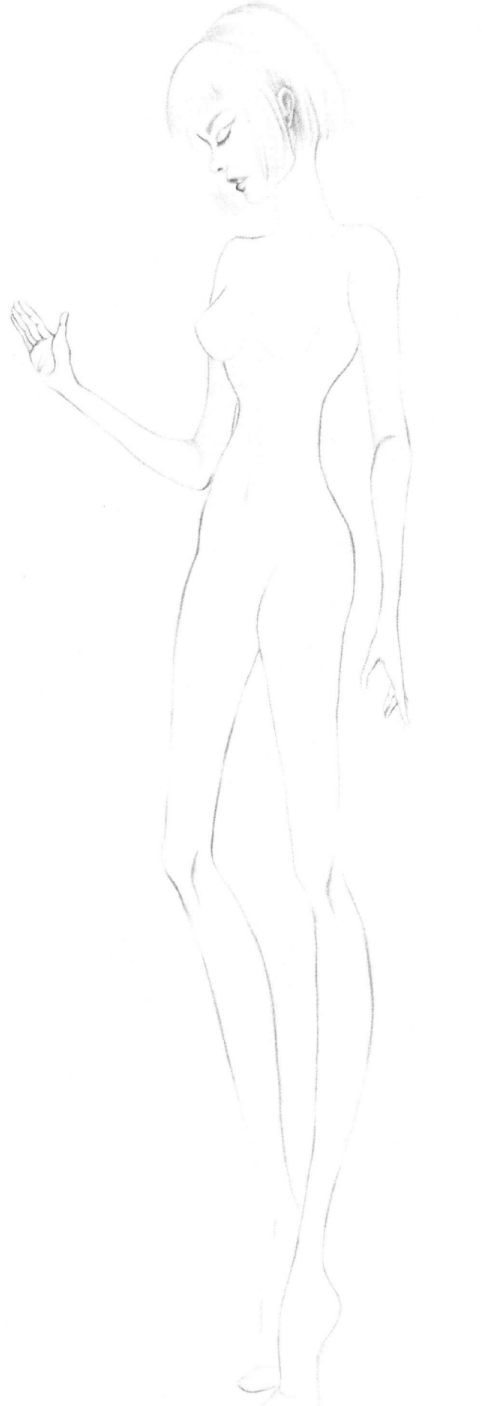

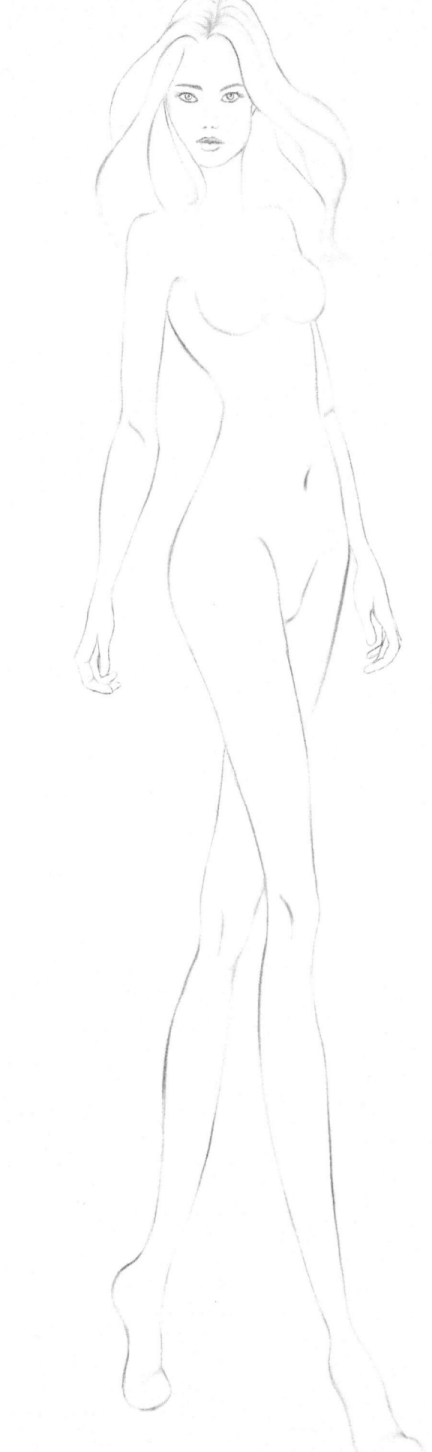

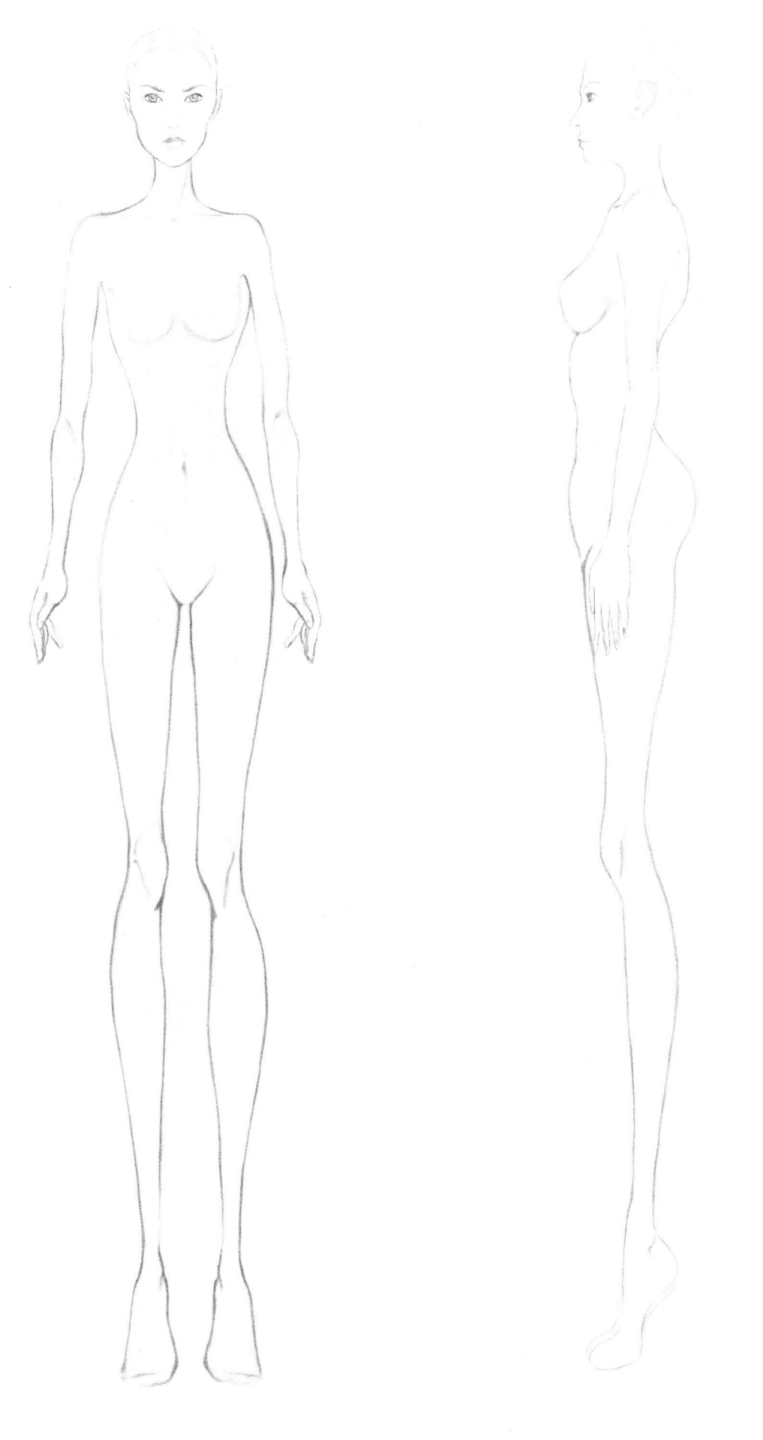

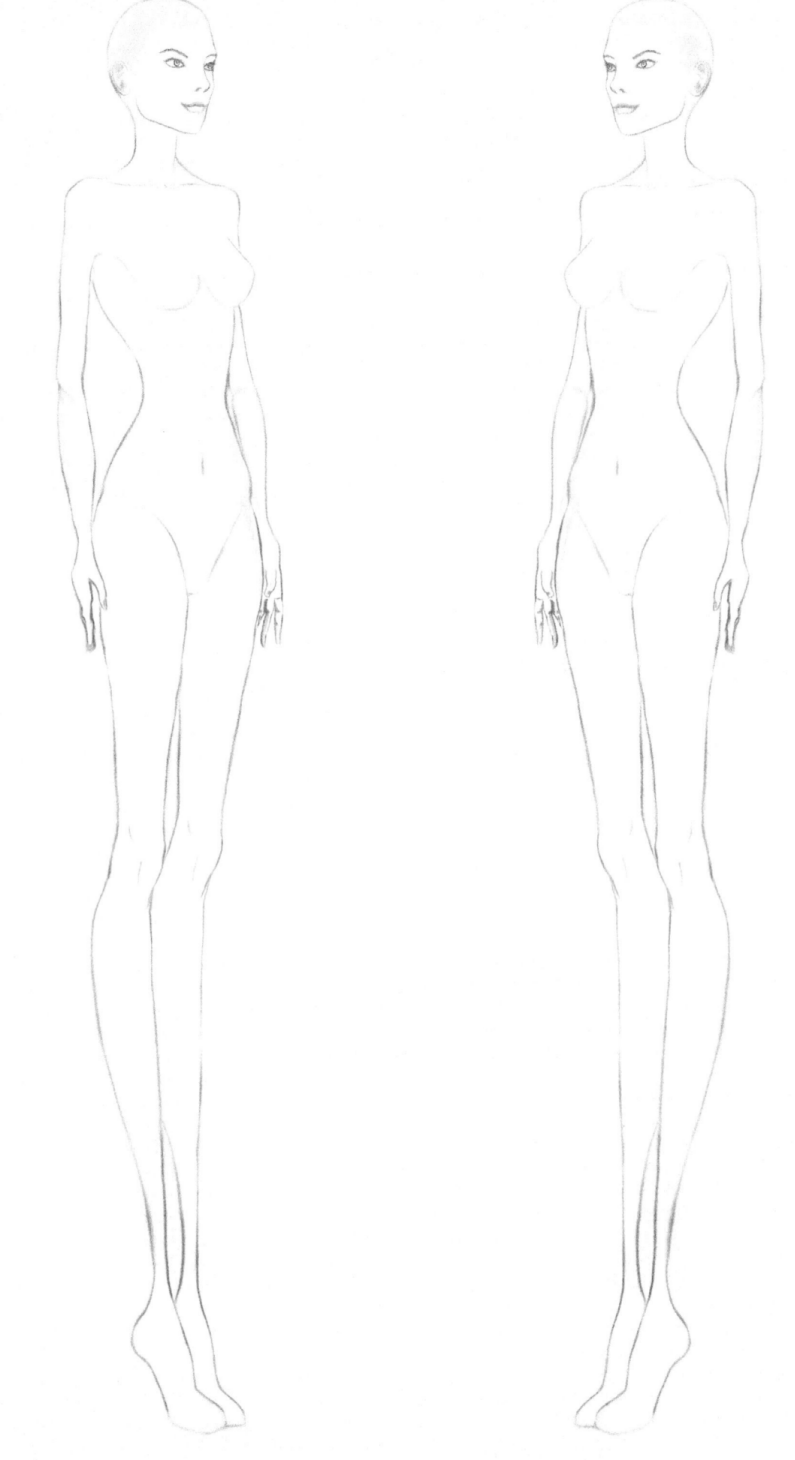

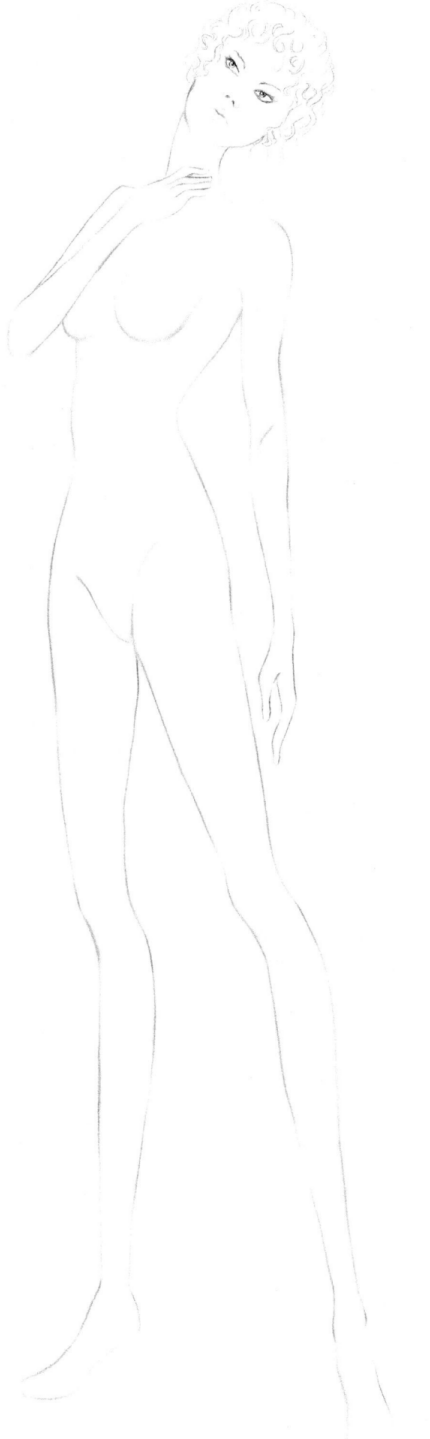

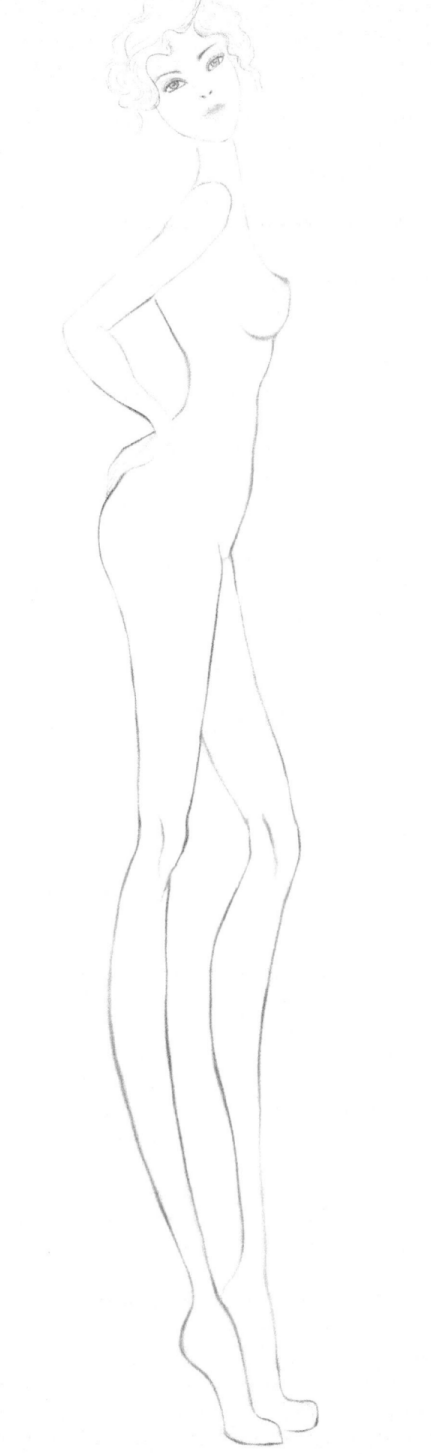

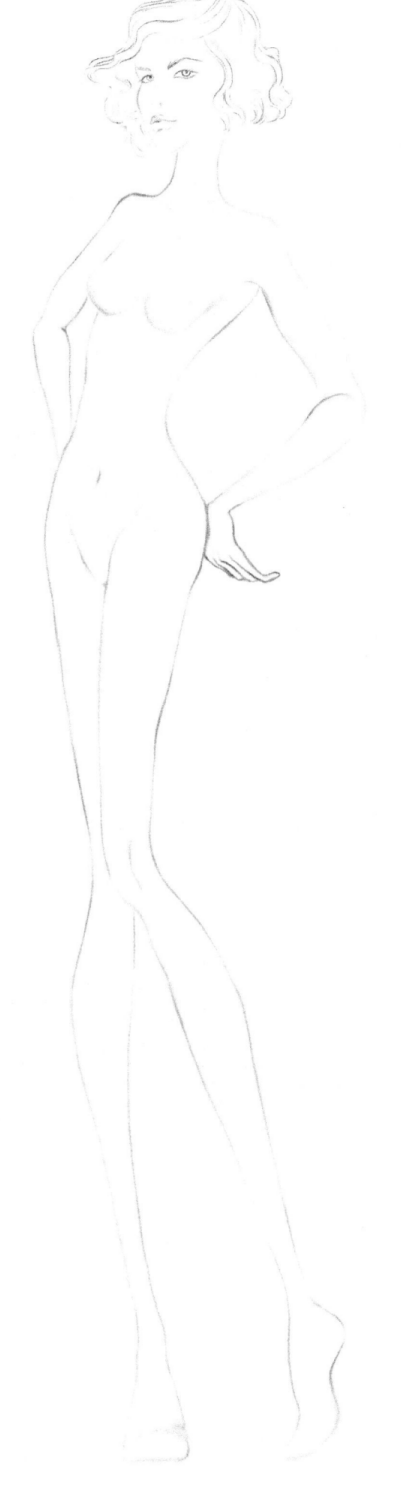

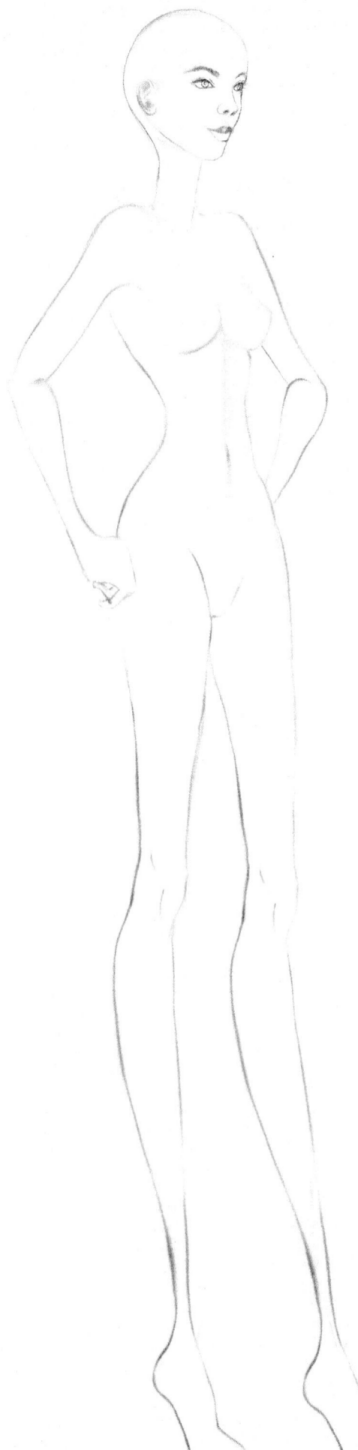

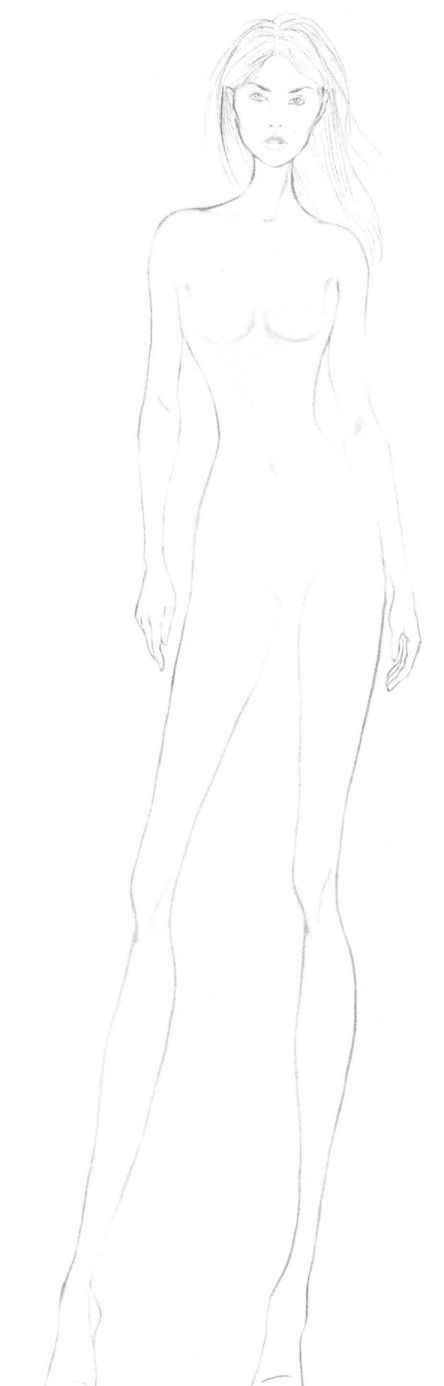

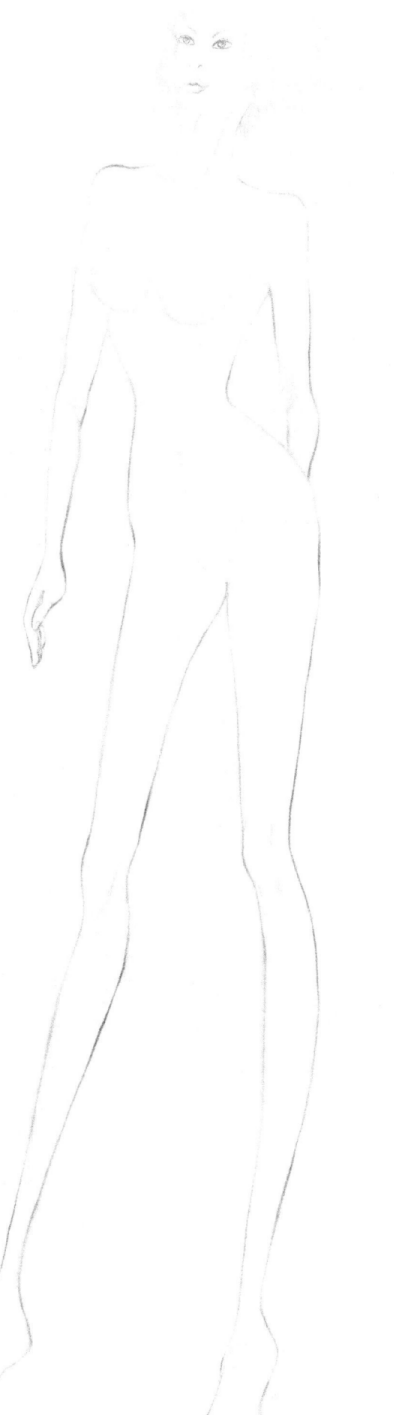

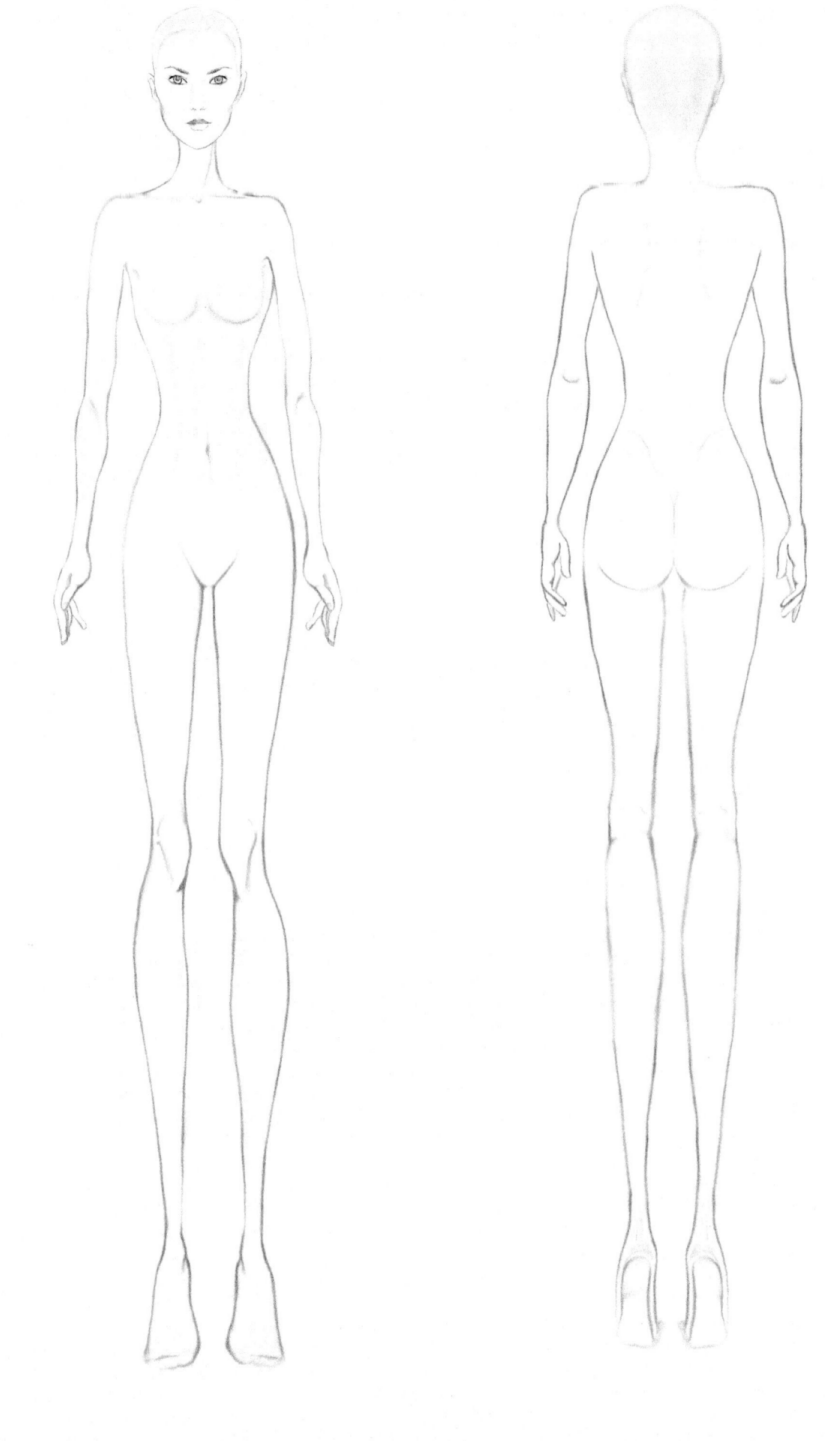

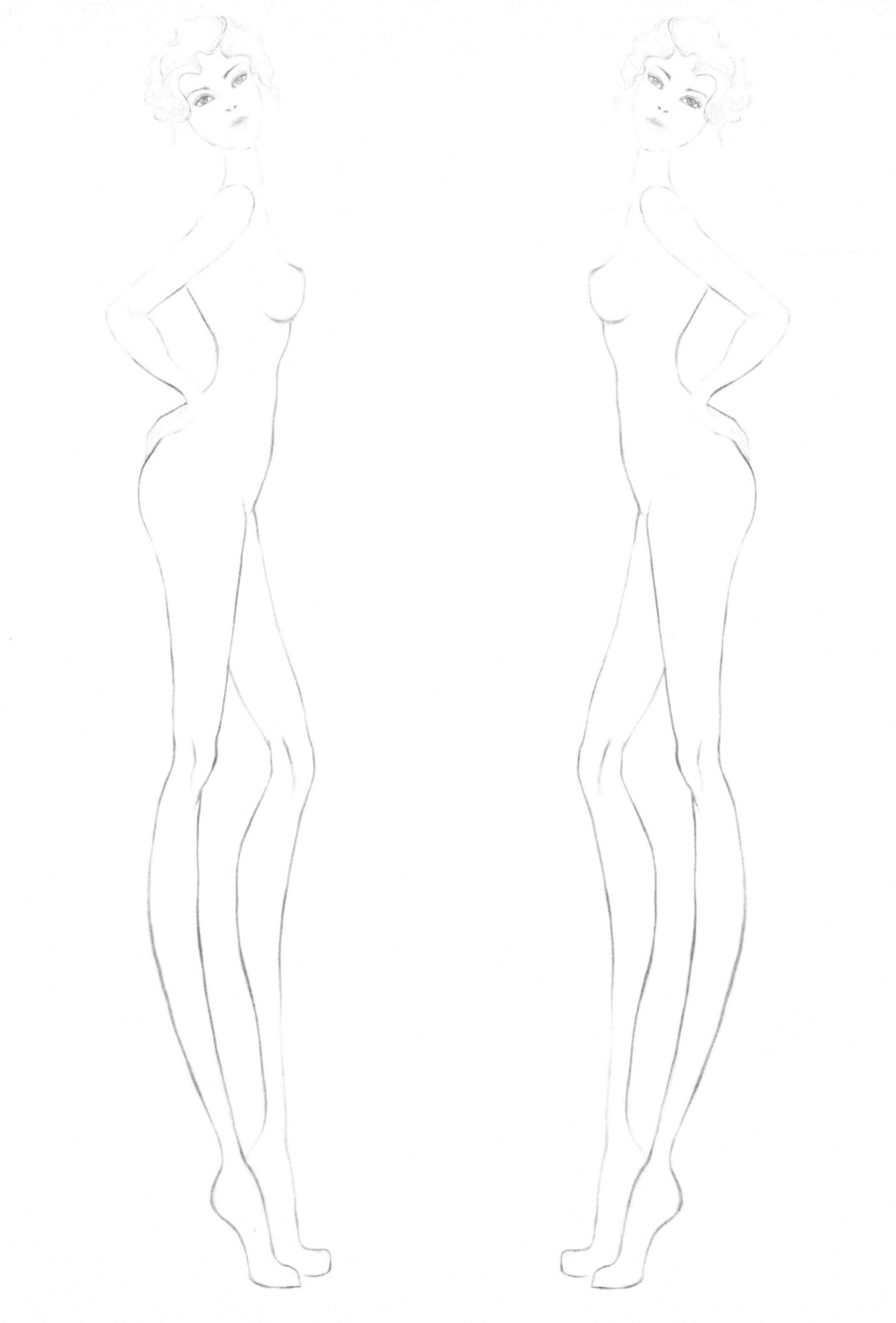

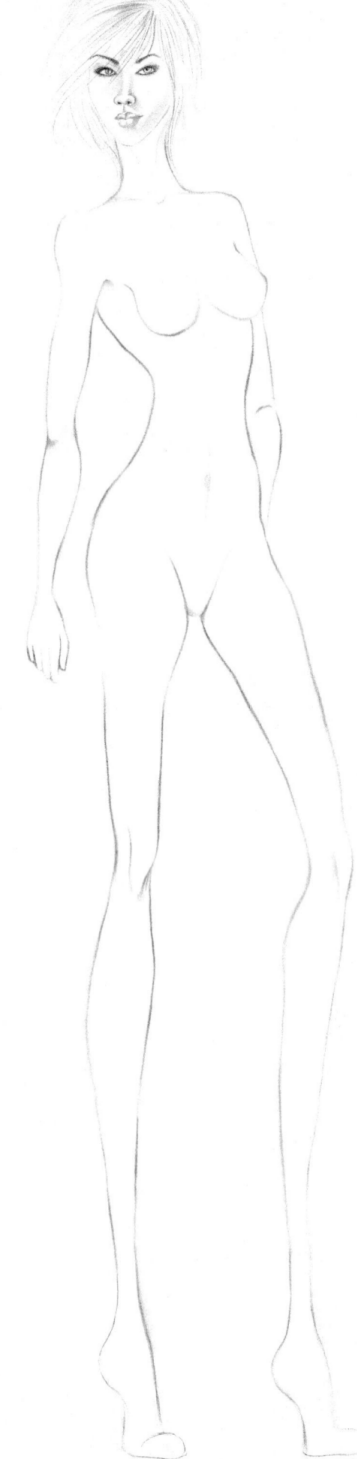

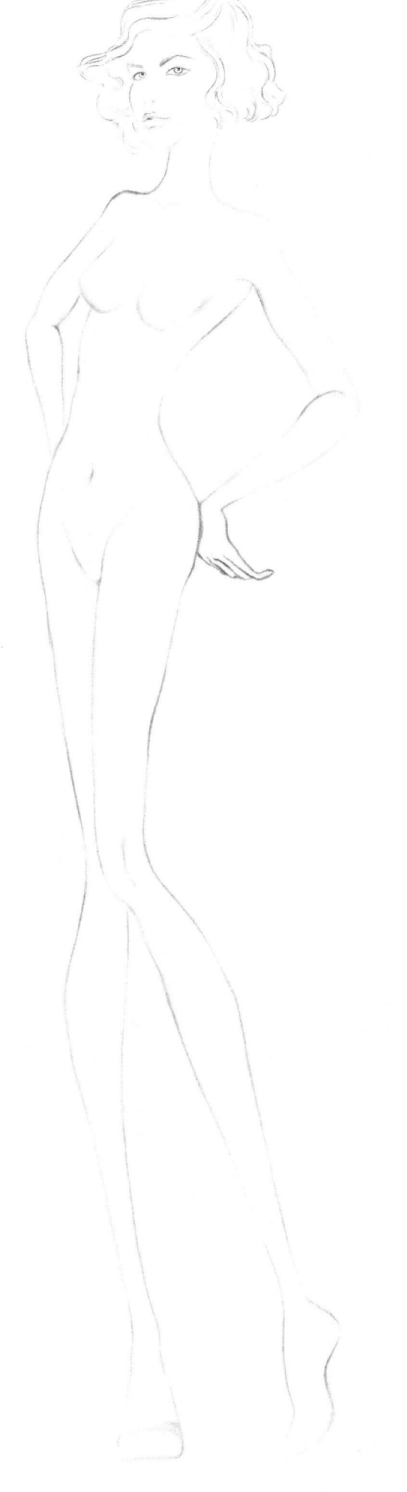

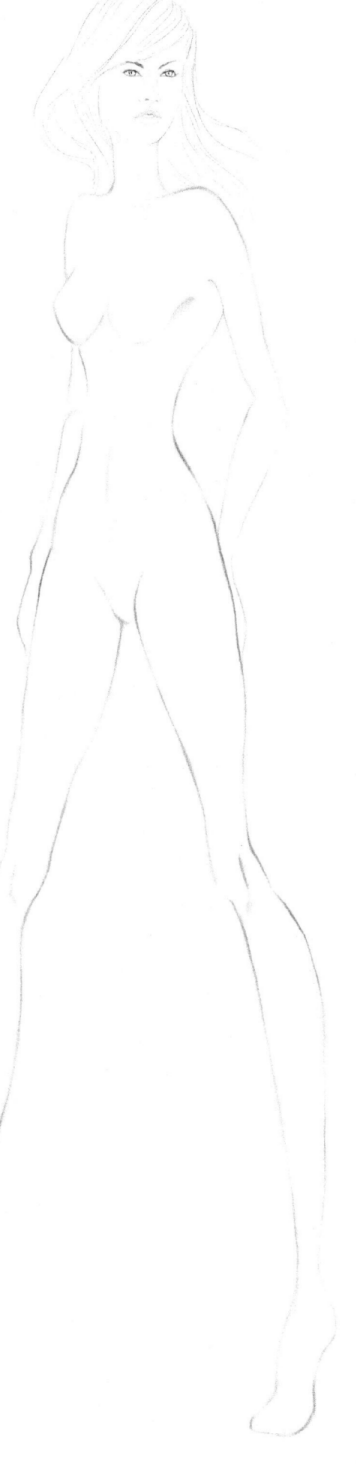

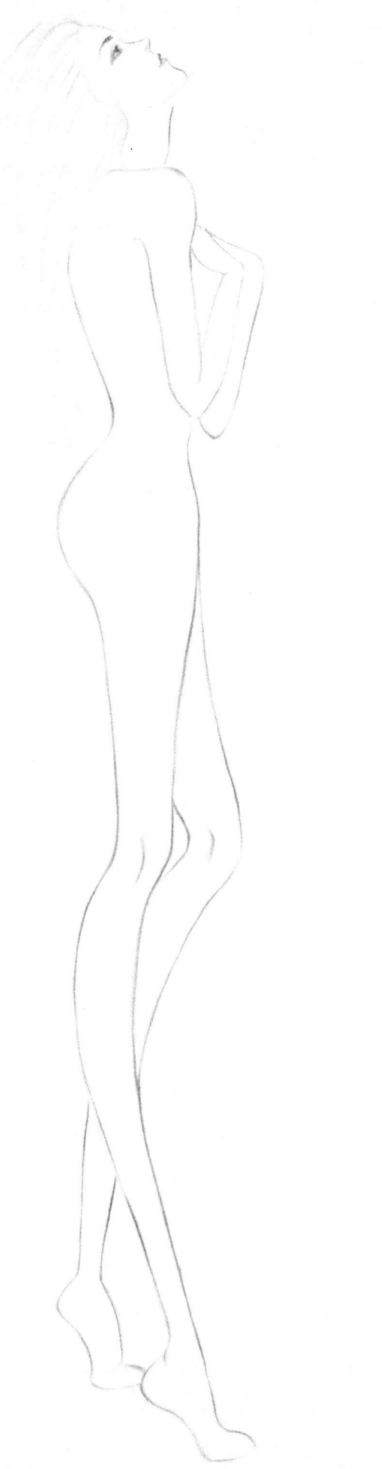

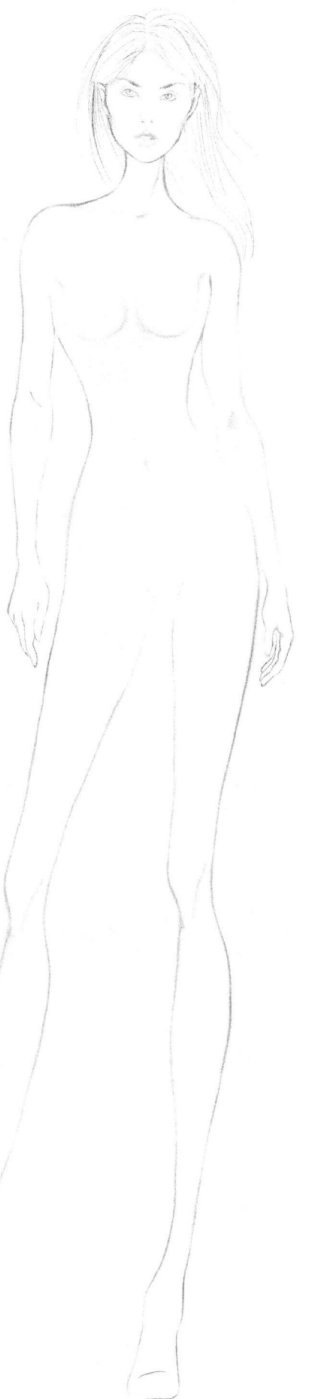

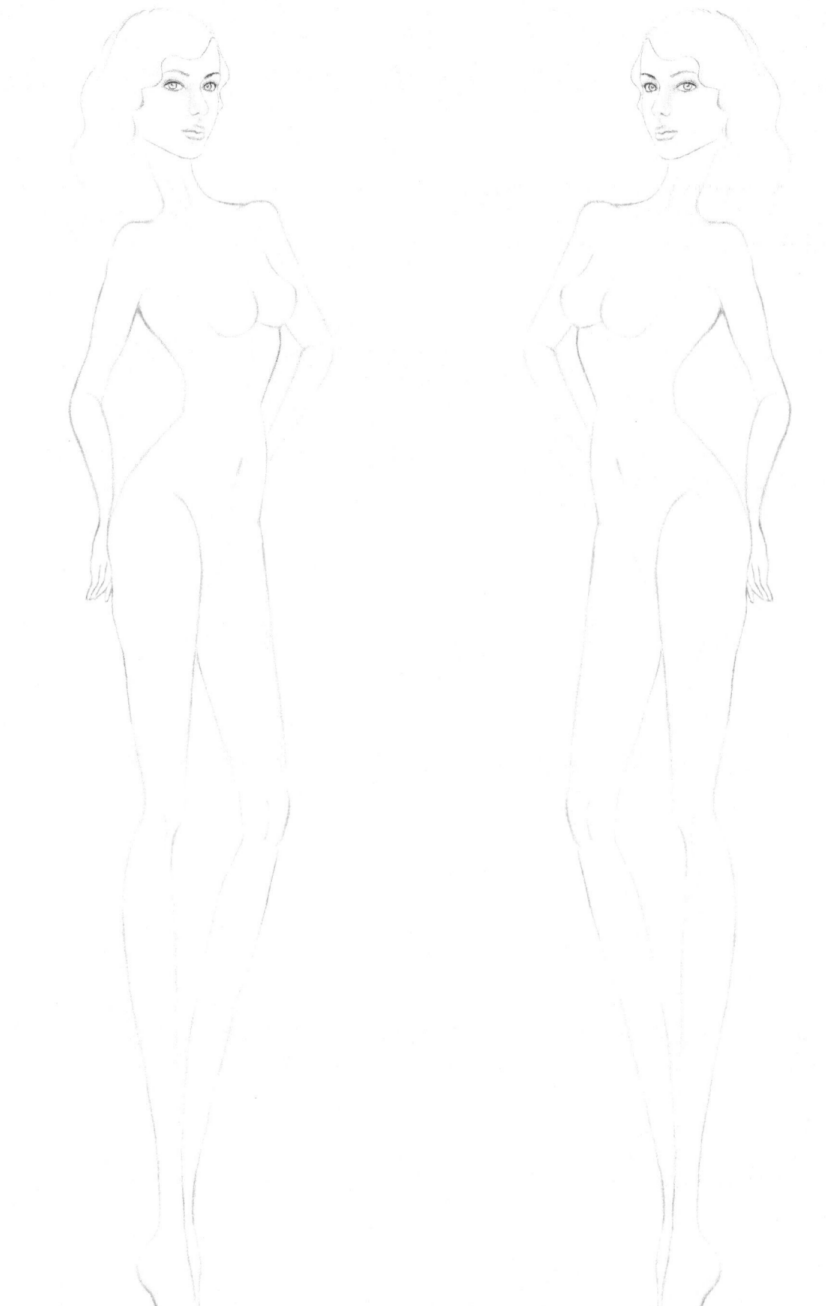

Printed in Great Britain
by Amazon